Evaluating Real Estate Investments as a Limited Partnership Investor: Three Case Studies
By Daniel Pessar

I0491047

Whether you are a young professional who has started to consider investing or a veteran investor interested in being more thorough in your analysis of real estate investment opportunities, this guide can help you to accomplish your goals. The guide features three fictional case studies which illustrate potential issues in real estate investments and describe some of the ways investors can think through these issues in order to make better investment decisions. Professionals rarely have the time, expertise, or risk-tolerance to acquire and manage private real estate investments. Instead, they usually invest with experienced operators who propose and carry out investment projects. The case studies below are representative of the kinds of deals you may have the opportunity to buy into at present or in the future. The case studies include a range of moving parts—including some details that sponsors might not share with investors—in order to provide the reader with a broad exposure to investment opportunities for limited partnership investors. After reading these case studies, you will be in a better position to evaluate investment opportunities, the sponsors proposing them, and your own unique profile as an investor.

The case studies are supposed to appear realistic but any details that resemble actual real estate professionals, firms, or deals is coincidental. Any unattributed pictures, including any pictures on the cover or back of the book, were sourced from Pixabay.com under the Pixabay License or were otherwise used with the permission of the owner. This guide does not contain legal advice.

Thank you for reading,
Daniel Pessar (dpessar@jd20.law.harvard.edu)

Table of Contents

Case 1: Journal Circle: Luxury multifamily redevelopment
This case study involves a multifamily redevelopment. Part of the offering memorandum analysis will include an evaluation of the deal "sponsor," the person or organization responsible for putting the deal together and making it a success. Following the commentary is a discussion of how to evaluate a sponsor's background and the incentive structure of the deal presented in the offering memorandum. While reading, consider the following questions:

1. Would you be interested in investing in this deal? If so, at what price and on what terms?

2. What concerns do you have about the deal? What information might you obtain that would satisfy those concerns?

3. What concerns do you have about the deal sponsor and what information might you obtain that would get you comfortable with the sponsor?

Overview – Sponsor Information – Business Plan – Exhibits – Pre-commentary Notes – Commentary – Post-commentary Notes

<u>Overview</u>

Address: 15-29 Newton Street, New City, Empire State

Size: 86,000 square feet (92,000 square feet projected at project completion)

Current occupancy: 50%

Construction: ~1896

Purchase price: $15 million

Total project capitalization: $31.95 million

Equity being sought by sponsor: $19.29 million

Anticipated investment term: three years

Projected return to limited partners: 12.8%

Newton Street Multifamily Portfolio, New City, Empire State

JPKP Capital Partners is excited to present a unique jewel of a project, a redevelopment of one-of-a-kind residential units steps away from the newly-renovated Millenium transit hub in Journal Circle in the center of New City, Empire State. Located on a quiet, historic cul-de-sac, tucked away in between two conventional streets, these redeveloped historic properties will be unmatched in the market of new high-end apartments in the area. The cobblestone pavers on the narrow street are a testament to the heritage of the area and the re-imagined homes will be designed with a respect for history in mind. The project consists of eight existing neighboring properties (15, 17, 19, 21, 23, 25, 27, 29 Newton Street) totalling 30 units which will be redeveloped and expanded into 39 carefully crafted rental residences. The buildings have very large units (2,866 square feet on average) as well as roofs and decks that can be enclosed as of right (no zoning approval needed) and unused basements that can be converted to usable space. The redevelopment will add approximately 10% of living space as well as additional storage space (converted cellars, attics, and crawl spaces) for residents.

Sponsor Information

James Paul ("J.P.") Smith holds degrees from Harvard's architecture school and Boston University. Before co-founding JPKP Capital Partners he was a Managing Director at Gold 360 Capital, a regional mortgage brokerage. At Gold 360, Smith was twice the highest grossing broker of the year (2011, 2012). In addition to acting as co-head of JPKP, James is a managing director at Smith Commercial Real Estate.

Kim Patrick ("K.P.") Fisher holds JD and MBA degrees from Rutgers University. Originally from Los Angeles, Fisher was a Vice President, Sales & Trading at RBX where he focused on Residential Mortgage Backed Securities (RMBS) investments. Fisher and Smith are LP investors in six LP deals and have served as advisors to over fifty value-add real estate acquisitions.

Business Plan

This project will take advantage of the New City renaissance, especially after the completion of the newly-renovated Millennium transit hub. There is rising demand for high-end residential rentals and condos given the great transportation access to high-paying jobs in New York City and elsewhere. (A recent article estimated over 200,000 jobs paying at least $120,000 within a 30-minute door-to-door commute.) Although there are over 4,000 new, mostly high-rise apartments in the pipeline in addition to the recently-delivered 5,000 units, the product is almost all high-rise, generic units. This acquisition offers the opportunity to deliver something unique: spacious, boutique, low-rise units. The redeveloped units will average 2,358 square feet (ranging from 1,400 square feet to 3,800 square feet) and will feature luxury finishes and fixtures including—depending on the unit— washer-dryers, jacuzzi tubes, pet rooms, and modern kitchens.

Changes to the tax laws have driven increased demand in the Journal Circle area because of taxpayer flight from high tax jurisdictions. The limitation of state and local tax income tax deductions in the 2017 Tax Cuts and Jobs Act has made it even more expensive for high earners to live in jurisdictions with high income tax. New City boasts no city income tax and a relatively low state income tax. The real estate market is hot with taxpayers who are eager to file next year's taxes as New City residents but are not yet interested in purchasing a home before they are more settled. Many prospective buyers are also waiting on the sidelines until housing prices cool down from the peak prices currently demanded by sellers.

The property is under contract for an attractive price because the units need to be renovated and half of the units are not currently rentable because of required upgrades to electrical capacity. However, the zoning allows for the projected increase in unit count to 39 and all of the required upgrades in the "down" units would need to be performed even if there were not any building code violations. The other reason for the attractive price is an 80-year-old covenant favoring several public entities that requires these buildings to be owned by a single entity. This unique stipulation cannot be undone according to expert legal advice provided to the sponsor and now serves as a positive attribute since it has made the property available at a winning price. According to the legal advice received, neither condo nor co-op redevelopment will work at this site, leaving rental units as the only feasible residential use.

Since New City is in a no-fault eviction state, the sponsor will be able to non-renew existing tenants in order to redevelop the property with no rent control or eviction laws to prevent the landlord from taking possession at the end of the lease. The Sponsor was also able to negotiate seller financing, a $12.5MM take-back mortgage (83% LTV representing 45.9% of the project capitalization) for five years, interest-only, at 8% interest. This financing allows for no prepayment penalty after two years of timely interest payments and provides significant flexibility and cost savings as there are no fees, no reporting requirements, no principal payments, and no prepayment penalties for most of the loan term.

None of the buildings are included in any historic register but because the properties are in the Journal Circle Historic District, any substantial construction needs the pre-approval of the historic commission which meets twice per year. The commission is very development-friendly, especially to construction that preserves the existing building facades, an important design decision already made for the current project. The historic nature of the project will not be an issue operationally and will actually serve to enhance returns as renters will be attracted to the unique story and design of the project.

The sponsor proposes a sale of the property project in year five, assuming conditions are ripe in the investment sales market.

Exhibits

Exhibit 1: Journal Circle site location relative to transportation hub

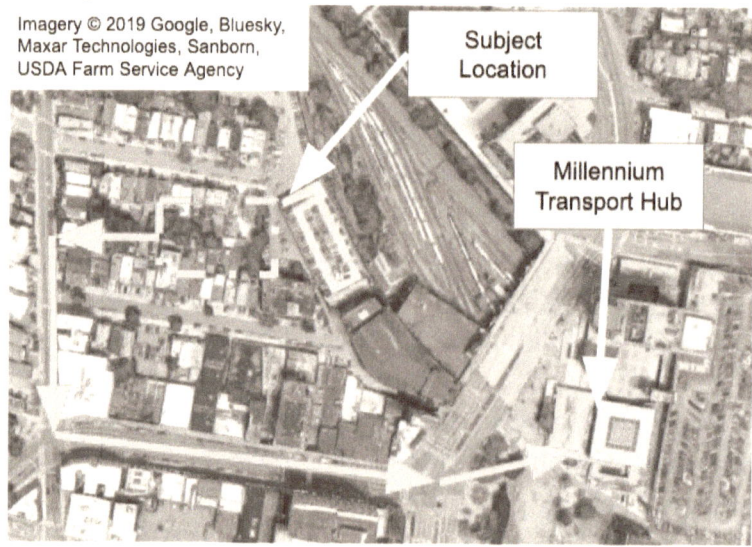

Imagery © 2019 Google, Bluesky, Maxar Technologies, Sanborn, USDA Farm Service Agency

Subject Location

Millennium Transport Hub

Exhibit 2: Journal Circle redevelopment sources and uses

Sources			Uses	
Sponsor Equity	$159,750		Purchase Price	$15,000,000
LP Equity	$19,290,250		Closing Expense	$1,000,000
Seller Financing	$12,500,000		Renovation	$10,000,000
Total	$31,950,000		Acquisition Fee	$450,000
			Working Capital	$500,000
			Interest Reserve	$5,000,000
			Total	$31,950,000

Exhibit 3: Journal Circle redevelopment assumptions and waterfall

Assumptions

Effective rent	$50 psf
Post-development Size	92,000 sf
Rent Growth	2%
Expense Growth	3%

Waterfall

	LP	Sponsor	Hurdle
Return of Capital	99%	0.5%	8%
Hurdle 1	80%	20%	12%
Hurdle 2	50%	50%	

Exhibit 4: Journal Circle redevelopment projected income and expense

	Year 1	Year 2	Year 3	Year 4
Rental Income	$110,000	$0	$3,400,000	$4,979,188
Concessions and Vacancy Loss	$11,000	$0	$340,000	$497,919
Net Rental Income	**$99,000**	**$0**	**$3,060,000**	**$4,481,269**
Property Tax	$350,000	$650,000	$669,500	$689,585
Insurance	$51,500	$53,045	$54,636	$56,275
Electric and Gas	$47,895	$49,332	$50,812	$52,336
Water	$26,608	$27,407	$28,229	$29,076
Property Management Fee	$4,950	$0	$153,000	$224,063
Construction Management Fee	$150,000	$300,000	$150,000	$0
Payroll and Contractor	$78,023	$80,363	$82,774	$85,257
Repair and Maintenance	$58,195	$59,941	$61,739	$63,591
Interest	$1,000,000	$1,000,000	$1,000,000	$0
Legal and Administrative	$41,200	$42,436	$43,709	$45,020
Other	$36,050	$37,132	$38,245	$39,393
Total Expenses	**$1,844,421**	**$2,299,655**	**$2,332,645**	**$1,284,597**
Net Operating Income	-$1,745,421	-$2,299,655	$727,355	$3,196,672
Exit Value @ 7.00% CAP			$45,666,739	
Exit Value @ 6.00% CAP			$53,277,862	
Exit Value @ 5.00% CAP			$63,933,435	
Project Unlevered Cash Flow	-$29,950,000	0	0	$50,349,019
Project Levered Cash Flow	-$19,450,000	0	0	$33,394,308

Exhibit 5: Journal Circle projected returns for LP and sponsor

<u>Returns Summary</u>

LP Total Cash Flow	-$19,351,875	$0	$0	$27,770,402
LP Cumulative Cash Flow	-$19,351,875	-$19,351,875	-$19,351,875	$8,418,527
LP IRR	12.8%			
LP Equity Multiple	1.44 x			
LP Peak Equity	$19,351,875			
LP Profit	$8,418,527			
Sponsor Total Cash Flow	-$98,125	$0	$0	$5,623,906
Sponsor Cumulative Cash Flow	-$98,125	-$98,125	-$98,125	$5,525,781
Sponsor IRR	285.6%			
Sponsor Equity Multiple	57.31 x			
Sponsor Peak Equity	$98,125			
Sponsor Profit	$5,525,781			

Note: The exhibits in this case present sponsor return metrics in addition to LP return metrics even though many sponsors are not very transparent about their own projected IRR and equity multiple. This lack of transparency occurs for at least two reasons. First, the sponsor does not want the LP to think that the sponsor's projected return is too generous. Second, IRR and equity multiple are not necessarily appropriate for sponsor returns because sponsor returns include performance driven payments. Just as one would not include a property management or project management fee in the sponsor IRR calculation, it can be argued that promote (carried interest) should likewise be omitted. As mentioned above, however, it is very important to understand how and when a sponsor makes money, if only to anticipate conflicts of interest and work to avoid them. At every stage of project success, it is good for a sponsor to look forward to more compensation. Absent these incentives, the sponsor may spend less time or energy on the project than necessary for a successful result.

Pre-commentary notes

....

....

....

....

....

....

....

....

....

....

....

....

....

Case Study 1 Commentary
Overview
The sponsor has certainly sourced an interesting deal: a development project that comes with seller financing in a booming real estate market. As always, development in a hot market can be risky because it can take years until the project is leased and/or sold and by that time the market

may have cooled off. That risk could be even more impactful here because the large unit sizes, historic district issue (discussed below), and low-rise nature of the offering are unlike most of the other residential inventory in the market. Sure, the uniqueness could result in high rents; however, the offering might miss the criteria sought by most renters in the market and that could make the project's leasing even more difficult in a downturn. For example, the largest unit is projected to be 3,800 square feet and the rents are assumed to be $50 per square foot, on average, growing at 2% per year. That translates to around $17,000 per month in rent in the lease-up year for the largest unit. At over $500 per night, renters with that budget might consider staying in a luxury hotel at some sort of extended-term discount until they are ready to buy a home. While the proposed units might be uniquely beautiful and well-located, high-end buyers will probably value safety and convenience to a degree not offered at these low-rise properties and high-rises might be a better fit for them. While developers tend to build condos over rentals in hot markets because the returns tend to be better, the sponsor must opt for rentals because of the easement mentioned above.

Sponsors

The fact that the offering memorandum does not mention previous deals and mentions Fisher and Smith acting in an advisory capacity makes it sound like this is their first deal. In fact, the advisory capacity might just consist of Smith's experience as a mortgage broker. Ultimately, it is not strictly necessary for two smart entrepreneurs to have deals under their belts in order to complete and operate the subject deal successfully. The question is: will you trust them given their experience profile? But that is not the only question. As discussed below, the question is also whether they should be managing certain functions that do require experience, like the Construction Management role. The offering does not make clear who will be receiving the $600,000 in construction management fees but assuming Smith and Fisher plan to handle the construction management themselves, their lack of experience in this area makes the role seem inappropriate for them.

Another concern about the sponsors relates to their career background. Although they have had some exposure to the real estate world, Fisher's Sales and Trading experience is not relevant to the proposed project. Furthermore, although Smith's experience in mortgage brokerage probably means he is proficient at raising capital and pitching deals, it does not mean he has any experience making a deal successful after closing, or even managing the acquisition due diligence. Finally, James's position as managing director at Smith Commercial Real Estate needs to be understood. Will James have time to operate this deal successfully given his other role? Is there a conflict of interest raised by this role?

Location
A prospective investor thinking about putting a significant sum into this project might consider visiting the property and looking at potential issues that could arise for this unique location such as odors and noise (from the nearby

train tracks or any commercial activity happening in the area), access (given traffic patterns at various times of the week), and crime rates which are often hyper-local in nature. Understanding the location, pricing, and features of the new residential units in the New City development pipeline is also important. Many of them will probably come into the market sooner than the proposed units and it would be helpful to better understand the kind of product competing for renters.

Redevelopment plan

The historic district approvals are a concern; even if application and approval has been simple in the past, one small hiccup could delay the project by six months or more because the relevant board only meets twice per year. Redevelopment can also present challenges in construction and permitting that new construction does not because of the existing conditions that have been at the property for over 100 years. All of the amenities, such as jacuzzi tubs, have unique requirements such as weight that the old floors and foundations will need to bear. (Hopefully these costs have been evaluated as part of the project planning.) As well, any soundproofing given the proximity to the transit hub could be complicated and expensive. Another significant issue relating to the pro forma is the physical structure of the project; since the portfolio is comprised of eight buildings instead of one, the portfolio may have eight separate boilers, roofs, and other capital items that drive up maintenance and capital costs. The best way to plan for these issues is while the property is under contract and before an acquisition contract deposit becomes nonrefundable. An investor should be confident in the sponsors' projection of potential costs and their ability to work through them successfully.

Pro forma

A quick analysis of the expenses shows that the sponsor did not do a thorough expense projection. Insurance, electric and gas, water, payroll and contractor, repair and maintenance, legal and administrative, and other expenses (seven of the eleven line items) were projected by taking the current expenses in the half-empty building and growing those expenses at 3% per year. While some costs could stay the same or even go down, most costs will likely rise given the increase in occupancy. As well, there are changing conditions at the building. The Offering Memorandum boasts that the newly renovated units will have washer/dryers and jacuzzis which are sure to consume huge amounts of water over and above the historical water usage; yet this pro forma reflects no such impact. With the increase in square footage, occupancy, and building value, the insurance expense is also likely to increase dramatically; again, no such impact is reflected in the pro forma.

Another issue that should be considered are the fees. Fees are always an emotional issue for sponsors who may own valuable equity interests but may be short on cash because of the long-term nature of the real estate business. One approach is to ask for the rationale behind each fee. For example, this project's $600,000 budget for construction management fees should probably be paid to a professional with a track record of successful project stewardship. Is the sponsor going to receive the entire amount? If so, does s/he have the requisite experience and bandwidth to be filling that function? Does the renovation budget include funds for construction management staff? If so, is this fee fee a double payment for construction management? Similar questions arise with regard to property management: is this fee (it appears to be 5% of net rental income) comparable to the fees charged by other property management companies in the market? What does the property get in the way of services for that money?

A successful deal will result in a big payday for the sponsor (over $5 million in performance compensation), a fact that should encourage an alignment of interests. But what happens if the market turns? In that case, if the project is unlikely to reach the first waterfall hurdle at 8%, the sponsor may have little reward to look forward to (he may have already received all or most of the $600,000 in development fees for moving forward with the project). One question not addressed in the document is whether there is a downside plan; perhaps renovating and leasing the 30 apartments without expansion of the project foot. Because the sponsor is putting up a mere 0.5% of the equity, it should not be assumed that there is an alignment of interest. And because the sponsor receives more in acquisition fees than his planned equity investment at closing, there is even less of a sense of skin in the game here. Most or all of the sponsors' time in a downturn might go to other projects or responsibilities given the lack of incentive to perform.

The sponsor can easily paint a profitable picture of the future by reducing the exit CAP (increasing the income multiple used to calculate the sale price), growing income projections faster than expense projections, and making unlikely assumptions about achievable rents as well as the costs required to maintain and improve the property. Below are two examples of adjustments made to sponsor projections to obtain more conservative (or more realistic) income and returns projections. The first analysis evaluates the effects of added expenses after year two—after the renovation:

Exhibit 6: Effects of expense increase after year two

	Current	+100K	+200K	+300K
LP IRR	12.8%	10.9%	9.0%	8.2%
LP Profit	$8,418,527	$7,068,527	$5,724,496	$5,184,496

The above table gives one example of adjusting the sponsor's pro forma in order to understand how a certain change in assumptions will impact returns projections. This table shows that an additional $300,000 in expenses after year two results in a ~460 basis point reduction in LP IRR, a very significant drop. Remember, the pro forma gives no indication that the water expense will be reimbursed by tenants and all that water that was not projected in the pro forma will need to be paid for somehow. While it might be hard for an LP to shake the current "12.8% IRR" number from his/her head, this is the emotional work involved in evaluating investments: reflect on the numbers that result from your reasonable investigation and calculations, not on any numbers that rely on faulty assumptions or calculations. Large increases in water alone could reach over $100,000 per year. If your analysis yields $200,000 in added expense, the question is yours to decide: given the risks, my alternative investment choices, and the possibility of just doing nothing, is a projected 9.0% IRR for this deal worth the substantial risks involved? Investors will examine their other investment options (perhaps a high credit NNN property or municipal bond) and decide whether the additional projected return is worth the additional deal risks, reduced liquidity of the real estate asset, and locked-in nature of the limited partnership investment.

The second analysis evaluates the project returns assuming a one year delay in project completion:

Exhibit 7: Returns summary with one year delay of project

Adjust Cash Flow (1 Year Delay)	-$19,450,000	$0	$0	$0	$33,394,308
Returns Summary					
LP Total Cash Flow	-$19,351,875	$0	$0	$0	$28,248,436
LP Cumulative Cash Flow	-$19,351,875	-$19,351,875	-$19,351,875	-$19,351,875	$8,896,561
LP IRR	9.9%				
LP Equity Multiple	1.46 x				
LP Peak Equity	$19,351,875				
LP Profit	$8,896,561				
Sponsor Total Cash Flow	-$98,125	$0	$0	$0	$5,145,872
Sponsor Cumulative Cash Flow	-$98,125	-$98,125	-$98,125	-$98,125	$5,047,747
Sponsor IRR	169.1%				
Sponsor Equity Multiple	52.44 x				
Sponsor Peak Equity	$98,125				
Sponsor Profit	$5,047,747				

The above exhibit makes a different change to the model assumptions and presents the results. Instead of adding expenses after year two, this exhibit presents the results from a one year delay in the project completion schedule. Among other impacted metrics, this one year delay results in a decline in projected LP IRR from 12.8% to 9.9%.

Commentary Summary

As with any deal, the investor needs to be satisfied with the projected return given the risks presented. It seems clear that the expense projection figures in the sponsor's pro forma are too low. In response to concerns raised about underwriting, a sponsor might be willing to change the fee structure to offset the lower anticipated returns. However, issues in the pro forma could indicate a potential for fraud or negligence and a shrewd investor might decide to pass on the deal on any terms after an investigation of the projections.

Evaluating Sponsor Background and Incentives, an Overview

Background

Some key traits that you might look for in a sponsor's background include:

(1) Commitment to the industry. Successful entrepreneurs can apply their ability to bring together resources and people in a variety of circumstances and industries. However, many people need to be committed to an industry—at least for a period—in order to get to the level of familiarity and expertise to do deals successfully. Might this person be off to the next industry before the business plan is successfully completed? (Of course, as long as the sponsor could successfully operate the deal, that would not matter, but the potential lack of attention and time spent on the deal might result in a suboptimal outcome.)

(2) Bandwidth. Think about the other projects and responsibilities that the sponsor including an unrelated day job, other properties under management, and potential projects in the pipeline. In addition to responsibilities, consider how much the person wants to work. Is this a post-retirement gig of an industry expert who might be tired of working? If so, can they be trusted to do the work necessary to save a project in distress?

(3) Good relationships and reputation. Lawsuits, bankruptcies, and scandals are the kinds of things that can lead to a loss of investor funds and sponsors with a history of conflict might not be the best stewards of capital. But great sponsors are sometimes caught in conflict and may need to pursue legal avenues in order to protect investor

funds. Ultimately, a pattern of working productively with a variety of vendors and industry insiders—especially those without reputation issues themselves—usually indicates that the sponsor has operational experience and the relationships necessary to mitigate risks, move quickly, and create value in his or her area of focus. Obtaining and checking references is a great way to obtain more information about the sponsor.

Incentives

Incentives are paramount in ensuring that a sponsor will provide time and attention to a project after closing. There are endless commitments that may compete for a sponsor's attention including new project pitches, problems at other projects under management, and personal commitments. While it might be convenient to assume that the sponsor will certainly want to make this project a success, it is important to consider what might happen under a variety of circumstances. After the sponsor earns an acquisition fee and is facing a development project in distress, the chances of earning a performance income (the "promote") by reaching the waterfall hurdles may be nearly impossible. The sponsor's time might be more profitably spent cultivating new projects rather than fighting day and night to get the highest possible returns for existing investors in the distressed project. The sponsor might not visit the site as often, may not work as aggressively to find great tenants, and might not run every bid as tightly as possible to extract the most value for the investors.

Of course, the more equity the sponsor has invested in the project up front, the more the sponsor will see himself or herself as one of the investors. Because sponsors with "skin in the game" will tend to work harder for the limited partners, institutional partners working with even the highest-quality sponsors on the best-credit deals often insist that the sponsor put a substantial amount of money in the projection. However, because many sponsors want to reduce their risks, or may not have access to liquid assets, many sponsors putting together deals will attempt to put up only a nominal amount of their own equity, if any. Investors beware.

An analysis of incentives is even more important in small deals because of the different incentive results. Although a small deal could result in a very high rate of return to the sponsor upon successful exit, the amount of money might be small as compared to other deals the sponsor might do. For example, if several years of work on a deal in California would reward a sponsor with a $500,000 promote at disposition, the investor might see this as adequate incentive to perform. But if the sponsor has a history of doing deals with $500,000 or more in acquisition fees in Florida—paid upfront before any post-closing work is done—the sponsor may drift towards putting together deals in Florida rather than spending all of the necessary time in California needed to operate that deal successfully.

Post-commentary Notes

....

....

....

....

....

....

....

....

....

....

....

....

....

....

Case 2: Off-market commercial property: Retail and industrial package

This case study involves the purchase of two off-market commercial properties. The analysis following the deal commentary includes a discussion of types of information generally contained in offering memorandums. While reading, consider the following questions:

1. Would you be interested in investing in this deal? If so, at what price and on what terms?

2. What concerns do you have about the deal? What information might you obtain that would satisfy those concerns?

3. Which information contained in the investment proposal contains a potential weakness in the deal or a potential red flag? What do you learn from these pieces of information and what do you still not know for sure?

Overview – Business Plan – Exhibits – Pre-commentary Notes – Commentary – Post-commentary Notes

Overview

Property	Retail Strip Mall	"Flex" Industrial Property
Address	580 NE 125th St, North Miami, FL 33161	1177 NW 81st St, Miami, FL 33150
Size	100,000 square feet	472,000 square feet
Current occupancy	0%	100%
Construction / Renovation	1945 / 1980	1977 / 2005
Purchase Price	$50 million	$57.54 million
Total Capitalization	$51.5 million	$59.04 million
Limited Partner Equity	$50.47 million	$57.86 million
Projected Investment Term	1 year	4 years
Projected Return to LP	10.0% (unlevered)	

580 NE 125th St, North Miami, FL 33161, 100% vacant strip mall in an excellent Miami location

1177 NW 81st St, Miami, FL 33150, 100% leased to seller, Outdoor Innovations Unlimited

Platinum Equity Partners and Associates (PEPA) is proud to present a unique opportunity to purchase two rare assets in greater Miami from a seller eager to exit the real estate business. Both properties are being sold at a significant discount to market value. The first property, a 100,000 square foot strip mall is being sold vacant, an excellent situation for a property in such a strong market given its "main and main" location. The second property, a 472,000 square foot "flex" industrial property is also located right near Interstate Route 95 and will continue to be tenanted by the seller after acquisition (a sale-leaseback transaction). The seller's business is a regional recreational equipment and playground manufacturing and assembly business that has been serving customers successfully since 1977. The company boasts revenues above $50 million and a workforce of over 100 employees.

PEPA is planning to structure the ownership of both properties in parallel fashion, with the same equity structure and with the same investors. This will allow investors to benefit from the diversification of two different income streams from two different real estate asset classes, retail and industrial. This deal will allow investors to acquire well-located properties at an excellent price, allowing great value to be locked in at closing. The industrial tenant signed a NNN lease and expected retail tenants are expected to sign NNN leases as well, reducing the time the sponsor needs to spend managing the property and, as a result, the service costs to investors. Because the properties are located under five miles away from each other (less than 15 minutes by car), the same operations staff can be utilized to carry out the business plan at both properties.

Business Plan: Retail strip mall

The owner of the retail strip mall purchased it in 2014 after it became apparent that the property was going to become vacant. The anchor tenant, an electronic-goods retailer, rejected the lease in bankruptcy and all of the other tenants exercised their termination options which allowed them to terminate their leases with 12 months notice once the anchor tenant leaves the space. The seller is very familiar with the North Miami area and thought he could structure an attractive deal with a grocery chain to take the anchor space and then fill the rest of the space with higher-paying tenants. Unfortunately, the seller has struggled to execute on the plan since he has spent very little time on the deal given his focus on his large operating business. As a high-net-worth individual who purchased the property for cash, this deal was mostly a place to park his money and he was more interested in protecting his downside with a well-located piece of real estate than in the potential upside from the deal . The rents he collected in the first year of ownership (before the strip mall went dark) covered most of his expenses to date since a successful post-vacancy tax reassessment drastically reduced his operating expenses.

The property is extremely well-located at the corner of NE 125th Street and NE 6th Avenue and its neighboring tenants include 7-Eleven, Walgreens, Publix, CVS, Goodyear Tires, and Universal Spirits and Smoke Warehouse. The anchor space would be suitable for a grocer, gym, or school which can drive traffic to the property and allow for the rest of the spaces to be leased at more attractive rents. An aggressive leasing plan is projected to result in 75% occupancy within two years and 100% in three years. The property will benefit from the strong Miami economy and strong economic fundamentals nationwide.

Because of the property's potential, the sponsor is in the final stages of negotiating a pre-sale with a national owner of retail property, a private REIT called WIX Capital Fund 3, to sell the retail property once the anchor space and 40% of the remaining square footage (a total of 64% occupancy) has been leased to tenants of a certain credit quality. This sale is projected for one year after closing with one six-month delay option that the sponsor can elect to use. This attractive deal even anticipates no cash flow to the buyer for one year after closing because of a projected one year of free rent offered to new tenants. The price will be based on NOI as inferred from the leases signed with the non-anchor leases signed (the anchor tenant traditionally leases at a lower rate). The CAP rate applied will be 6.2%, 100 basis points above the market CAP rate of 5.2%, as adjusted based on 10 year Treasury rates (i.e., if Treasuries decline between the WIX contract and the sale by 50 bps, the CAP rate applied will similarly decline to 5.7%. Although the partnership should be able to sell for a higher price approximately one year later once the property is fully occupied (assuming CAP rates do not rise substantially), this contract allows for tremendous risk to be taken off the table early and a fantastic result— something to be celebrated in a market with the turbulence and geopolitical risk that we are experiencing today.

Business Plan: Industrial "flex" property

The industrial property is encumbered by an environmental land use restrictive easement which restricts residential activity and building activity without certain remediation efforts occurring first. The covenant was put into place by the Florida Department of Environmental Protection as a result of conditions that existed because of a historical manufacturing use at the site that caused certain chemicals to seep into the soil. Thankfully, this condition does not affect the business plan, which calls for managing the site as an industrial "flex" property over the long term and does not call for redevelopment as a residential site or otherwise—actions that would require expensive remediation efforts before breaking ground. All foreseeable tenant improvements such as installing new equipment in the building, renovating loading docks or office space, or repaving the parking lot are not affected by the restrictive covenant.

The current tenant is Outdoor Innovations Unlimited (OIU), owned and managed by Steven Stephenson and his family since 1988. The company was originally founded as Recreation for Children in 1977 and was rebranded after a merger with Stephenson's company in 1988. Following the merger, OIU moved its operations to the current location. The company has a steady, but shrinking, customer base and online retailing and new distribution channels have made the business much more challenging in recent years. Despite the challenges, OIU continues to sell to many regional distributors and has a great reputation throughout the United States and Canada. OIU still uses the entire space for its operations but now uses around half of the space for storage instead of manufacturing. Much of its machinery is no longer in use since it has found ways to outsource much of its assembly. The lease with OIU, to be assumed at closing, allows for termination by OIU with 12 months notice. Thankfully, the rent is below market, allowing for a successful deal whether the tenant remains in the space or vacates. The rent, although below-market, will provide a great return under the expected scenario of OIU staying put for the near term given its familiarity with the space and the great lease terms it enjoys.

The market for industrial space is booming nationwide as companies compete for regional and "last-mile" distribution facilities. This property offers a fantastic opportunity to manufacturers and retailers alike because of its (1) five-minute drive to Interstate Route 95, (2) great layout for "flex space," allowing for an office plus storage/distribution/manufacturing use, (3) unused acreage on-site which allows for further development in case a tenant needs to grow or better-utilize the property, and (4) location less than 8 miles away from the Miami Port, one of the busiest ports in the world. The property's facade has been very well maintained which adds to the curb appeal in case re-leasing is necessary.

While there is plenty of upside potential by upgrading the property and attracting a national tenant, a conservative case has been modeled: collecting an attractive return on the investment and selling at a market CAP rate at the end of year four. Depending on re-tenanting efforts and market conditions, the sponsor might consider taking debt on the property as well.

As of now, the entire project—including both properties—is being planned as an unlevered investment in order to reduce risks to investors, allow for more equity to be invested, and to increase project flexibility. The sponsor will consider a structure involving appropriate leverage to increase returns and decrease the required equity investment.

Model assumptions

Our enclosed model, based on conversations with local brokers and tenants, assumes the following:

Industrial: in order to account for a possible lease renegotiation or incentives needed to attract a new tenant in the space, 50% of annual rents and expense reimbursements are modeled as a concession in years three and four of the project.

Retail: one year of full vacancy is assumed after closing followed by one year of free rent given to tenants. The model assumes an anchor tenants and 40% of other tenants (by square footage) will be signed at the end of year one. One year following, the model assumes 100% occupancy at market rents. Market and lease rents are assumed to increase annually by 3% and expenses by 2%. Tenants are assumed not to pay property tax during their free rent periods.

Among other benefits of purchasing the properties together is the ability for the industrial property net income to fund the losses at the retail property after closing. The large rents coming from the seller-tenant of the industrial property will allow for no large working capital allocation to be taken to offset losses at the vacant retail properties.

Exhibits
Exhibit 1: Retail property area map

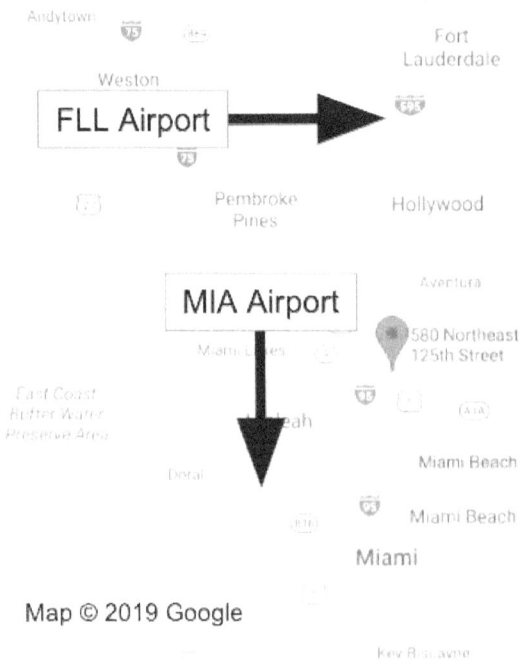

Map © 2019 Google

Exhibit 2: Retail property neighborhood map

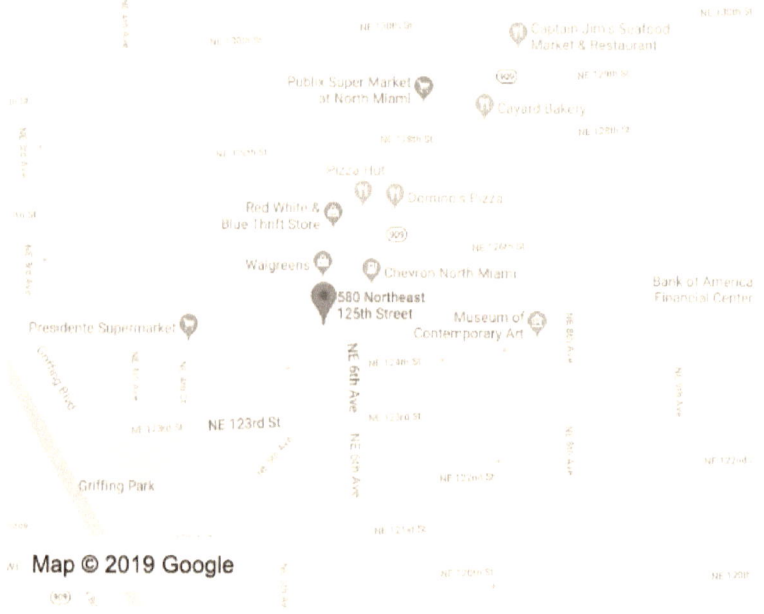

Map © 2019 Google

Exhibit 3: Retail property rent roll

Unit #	Retail Type	Square Footage	Market Rent	Status
100	Anchor	35,000	$1,050,000	Vacant
101a	Non-anchor	8,000	$400,000	Vacant
101b	In line retail	8,000	$400,000	Vacant
101c	In line retail	8,000	$400,000	Vacant
102	In line retail	4,400	$220,000	Vacant
103	In line retail	3,606	$180,300	Vacant
104	In line retail	3,600	$180,000	Vacant
105	In line retail	3,150	$157,500	Vacant
106	In line retail	2,640	$132,000	Vacant
107	In line retail	2,386	$119,300	Vacant
108	In line retail	1,880	$94,000	Vacant
109	In line retail	1,800	$90,000	Vacant
110	In line retail	1,800	$90,000	Vacant
111	In line retail	1,800	$90,000	Vacant
112	In line retail	1,800	$90,000	Vacant
113	In line retail	1,800	$90,000	Vacant
114	In line retail	1,800	$90,000	Vacant
115	In line retail	1,600	$80,000	Vacant
116	In line retail	1,300	$65,000	Vacant
117	In line retail	1,280	$64,000	Vacant
118	In line retail	1,260	$63,000	Vacant
119	In line retail	1,178	$58,900	Vacant
120	In line retail	960	$48,000	Vacant
121	In line retail	960	$48,000	Vacant

Exhibit 4: Retail property space summary

Assumptions- Retail

Rent - Retail Anchor	$30	psf
Rent - Retail Other	$50	psf
No. Retail Units	26	
Retail Size	100,000	sf
Anchor Retail Size	35,000	sf
Other Retail Size	65,000	sf
Rent Growth - Retail	3%	
Expense Growth - Retail	2%	
PGI - Retail	$4,300,000	

Exhibit 5: Industrial property space summary

Assumptions- Industrial

Rent - Industrial	$11	psf
Industrial Size	472,000	sf
Rent Growth - Industrial	3%	
Expense Growth - Industrial	2%	

Exhibit 6: Industrial property area map

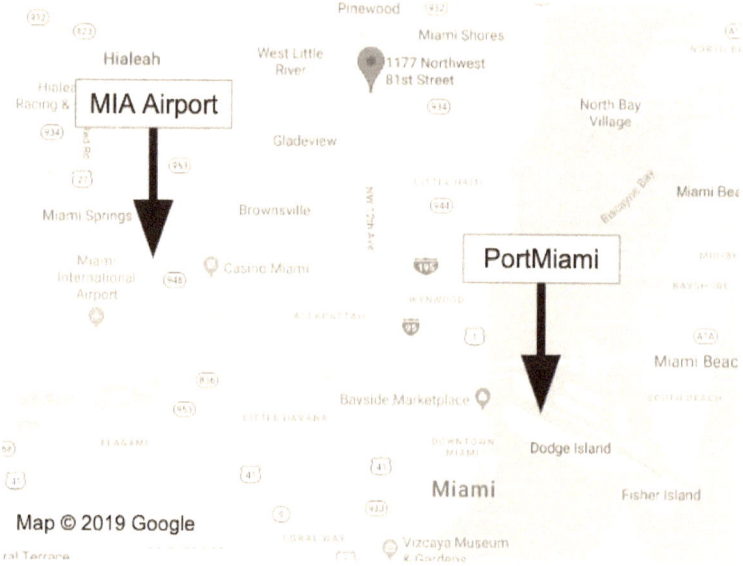

Map © 2019 Google

Exhibit 7: Industrial property neighborhood map

Map © 2019 Google

Exhibit 8: Outdoor Innovations Unlimited (OIU) marketing photo

Exhibit 9: Pro forma income and expense

Industrial Property	Year 1	Year 2	Year 3	Year 4	Year 5
Rental Income	$5,347,760	$5,508,193	$5,673,439	$5,843,642	$6,018,951
Property Tax Reimbursement	$1,020,000	$1,040,400	$1,061,208	$1,082,432	$1,104,081
Concessions and Vacancy Loss	$0	$0	$3,367,323	$3,463,037	$0
Net Rental Income (NRI)	$6,367,760	$6,548,593	$3,367,323	$3,463,037	$7,123,032
Property Tax	$1,020,000	$1,040,400	$1,061,208	$1,082,432	$1,104,081
Insurance	$204,000	$208,080	$212,242	$216,486	$220,816
Electric and Gas	$0	$0	$0	$0	$0
Water	$0	$0	$0	$0	$0
Property Management Fee (2% of NRI)	$127,355	$130,972	$67,346	$69,261	$142,461
Payroll and Contractor	$102,000	$104,040	$106,121	$108,243	$110,408
Repair and Maintenance	$23,460	$23,929	$24,408	$24,896	$25,394
Total Expenses	$1,476,815	$1,507,421	$1,471,325	$1,501,318	$1,603,160
Industrial: Net Operating Income	$4,890,945	$5,041,172	$1,895,999	$1,961,718	$5,519,872
				$71,686,653	
Retail Property					
Rental Income	$0	$0	$2,567,908	$4,839,688	$4,984,879
Concessions and Vacancy Loss	$0	$0	-$2,567,908	-$2,194,742	$0
Net Rental Income	$0	$0	$0	$2,644,946	$4,984,879
Property Tax - fully reimbursed	$800,000	$816,000	$832,320	$0	$0
Insurance	$80,000	$81,600	$83,232	$84,897	$86,595
Electric and Gas - none. NNN	$0	$0	$0	$0	$0
Water - none, NNN	$0	$0	$0	$0	$0
Property Management Fee (100k / 3%)	$100,000	$100,000	$100,000	$100,000	$149,546
Payroll and Contractor	$102,000	$104,040	$106,121	$108,243	$110,408
Repair and Maintenance- plug	$15,300	$15,606	$15,918	$16,236	$16,561
Security Services for Vacant Property	$150,000	$0	$0	$0	$0
Total Expenses	$1,247,300	$1,117,246	$1,137,591	$309,376	$363,110
Retail: Net Operating Income	-$1,247,300	-$1,117,246	-$1,137,591	$2,335,569	$4,621,768
Total NOI	$3,643,645	$3,923,926	$758,408	$4,297,288	$10,141,641

Exhibit 10: Pro forma post-waterfall returns distribution

Returns Summary

LP Total Cash Flow	-$108,329,717	$73,973,438	$4,940,348	$1,858,079	$52,084,622
LP Cumulative Cash Flow	-$108,329,717	-$34,356,279	-$29,415,930	-$27,557,852	$24,526,770
LP IRR	10.0%				
LP Equity Multiple	1.23 x				
LP Peak Equity	$108,329,717				
LP Profit	$24,526,770				
Sponsor Total Cash Flow	-$2,210,811	$1,509,662	$100,823	$37,920	$21,563,749
Sponsor Cumulative Cash Flow	-$2,210,811	-$701,149	-$600,325	-$562,405	$21,001,344
Sponsor IRR	97.5%				
Sponsor Equity Multiple	10.50 x				
Sponsor Peak Equity	$2,210,811				
Sponsor Profit	$21,001,344				

Pre-commentary Notes

....

....

....

....

....

....

....

....

....

....

....

....

....

....

Case Study 2 Commentary:

Retail Property:

Overview:

The City of North Miami is not the same as the City of Miami, it is several miles north of Miami and has a different economic, geographic, and demographic profile. Although there are certainly some benefits that accrue to cities adjacent to booming centers of commerce such as Miami, lumping these cities together gives the impression that the retail property location is better than it really is. The location may be very good relative to the neighborhood, but demographics will need to be understood in order to project how retailers will think about the opportunity. Retailers—and all businesses—try to avoid hotspots for crime (North Miami is known to have more than its fair share of violent crime) and nuisance traffic (perhaps the traffic coming from Universal Spirits and Smoke Warehouse is not conducive to a successful retail location), bringing down potential rents.

The property probably has promise and the possibility of a sale at 64% occupancy will certainly boost return potential on an IRR basis. However, investors will need to think about their own investment priorities and tax situation as sometimes a longer horizon with increased profits but lower IRR will make more sense for an investor. A longer term investment can save the time and distraction involved in constantly redeploying capital and may make investments more efficient by pushing off returns realization to the future.

One important question for the sponsor is why the properties are being lumped into one offering. Just because the seller is the same does not mean the same investors will be interested in both deals. The deals look different in terms of asset class, investment horizon, business plan, and prospective tenant credit. One possibility is that grouping the deals is a strategy meant to make the industrial property seem more attractive than it actually is by grouping it with a "value-add" deal with the potential for a quick exit and high IRR. Maybe the seller required the sponsor to purchase both properties in a package.

But even if an investor was open to such an arrangement, it is important to remember that most of the deal horizon will involve owning the industrial property and not the retail property (because the retail property might be sold 12 months after acquisition). While the prospect of receiving a significant chunk of the investment back in twelve months is attractive, investors must remember that in a downturn, the ability to sell the less-attractive industrial property at an attractive price will be hit much harder than the ability to sell the retail property since the retail property is expected to have a tenant mix with a much better credit profile. A quick analysis of the pro forma cash flows of the two properties on a stand alone basis reveals the stark differences between them (10.66% IRR versus 37.07% IRR for a blended 16.08% IRR at the deal level), even when taking the sponsor pro forma at face value. Now we know why the sponsor presented only the combined IRR in the investment summary table at the beginning of the offering memorandum.

	Year 1	Year 2	Year 3	Year 4
Project Unlevered Cash Flow	-$110,540,527	$75,483,100	$5,041,172	$1,895,999 $73,648,371
Industrial Unlevered Cash Flow	-$59,040,527	$4,890,945	$5,041,172	$1,895,999 $73,648,371
Retail Unlevered Cash Flow	-$51,500,000	$70,592,155		

The retail pro forma might be too aggressive, a fact that might impact future NOI and could also undermine efforts to sell the property quickly to the prospective buyer. The pro forma assumes that two years of vacancy will adequately represent necessary tenant improvement allowances and a potential free rent package (not to mention broker fees). These assumptions must be substantiated by looking closer at the market for retail space.

<u>Industrial property:</u>
Overview:
It is not safe to assume OIU will remain in the space or that if it remains in the space it will agree to maintain the same lease terms. On the contrary, given OIU's financial challenges, investors should assume the tenant will vacate in the near term, maybe even giving its termination notice on the day after the acquisition date. OIU may even be staying in the space for the sole purpose of trying to get a high price for the building (by selling it as fully occupied real estate rather than as 100% vacant space). Although $50 million in revenues may give a sense of a company's size, it gives no indication of its financial health, especially considering our knowledge of the company's declining fortunes. Employee-count just gives a small indication of its expenses, not its solvency or stability. The sponsor should have renegotiated the lease with the seller as part of the acquisition conversation and included some credit enhancement (e.g., large security deposit, credit-worthy guarantor, pledge of collateral) even in exchange for a higher purchase price or lower rent.

The use of the phrase "sale-leaseback" in the offering memorandum may be technically correct but is not in the spirit of a sale-leaseback transaction which tends to be quite similar to providing financing to the seller-owner in exchange for a long-term lease. Here, because the tenant does not appear to have strong credit at all and can exit with 12 months notice, this looks more like a traditional sale that comes along with an unenforceable promise of some rent after closing. There was not even a mention of a personal guarantee from the seller or his family. Even if there were, however, a buyer should need some guarantees that that guarantor is solvent and has adequate wealth to service any payments from a lease in default (the claim that the seller is a "high-net-worth individual" should be substantiated if his guarantee is used in any part of the deal). As far as we know, OIU can declare bankruptcy after the building sale closes and not even pay rent for the 12 months remaining on the lease after a lease termination notice is executed.

The proposal to use the property for distribution or "last-mile" delivery is certainly an interesting idea but it is not more than an idea. There is no indication that the sponsor has had conversations with any potential distributor or broker or any prospective tenant at all. (This makes sense, given the sponsor's "expectation" that the tenant will remain for at least several years, an assumption that also does not seem to be based on good facts.) The property also has major issues that any investor should consider because they may reduce future profit potential at the property: (1) the environmental issues will be worrisome for any tenant concerned about long-term utilization of the site, safety of employees, liability, and reputation in the community,[1] (2) the existence of unused machinery at the facility might be expensive to remove if the current tenant vacates, and (3) despite the mention of a well-kept

---

[1] The sponsor lists "further development" potential at the site as an advantage to potential tenants but that seems to contradict its description of the restrictive covenant on the site. How can the acreage be developed without solving the environmental issues? If only the building—but not the acreage—is subject to the restrictions, which kinds of tenants will be excited about developing the acreage while not touching the existing facility?

facade, a new tenant might require very expensive tenant improvements after decades of occupancy by the same tenant. This issue becomes more pronounced when investors consider that the 100%-occupied property might be best-suited for multiple tenants in the future, resulting in even more construction required to reposition the property. If the best strategy is for multiple tenants to lease space at the property, it could take even longer to find tenants and prepare their spaces. Moreover, even the proximity to the Miami Port (indeed, one of the busiest ports in the world) needs to be understood in the context of the business plan. Certainly the fact that the Miami Port's activity mostly comes from cruise traffic is not helpful to most commercial landlords.

Even if the rent is truly below-market and the required concessions and tenant improvements will not preclude a good return to investors, the environmental liability will need to be understood. Depending on the relevant federal, state, and/or local laws, environmental liability can follow owners forever (by statute, without the ability to remove the liability through contract) even if the owner had nothing to do with the introduction of the environmental condition in the first place. As well, a bank may be less willing to lend against the property given the environmental challenges and its lack of a long-term lease. This financing situation could turn away potential buyers. The next area of concern is the capital plan. Given the expected lack of financing in the first few years of the deal, the project will need to be funded with equity. If the industrial tenant stops paying rent right after closing, or gives a termination notice, one or more years of vacancy could follow as well as required tenant improvement costs that need to be funded in the interim. Vacancy in year two alone could cost $2.4 million or more, not including lease-up expenses and commissions at both properties which could far exceed $1 million. But the project's capital plan only includes $500,000 for working capital. How will the potential shortfall be funded? If the sponsor and investors cannot, or will not, fund a capital call, the property could lay vacant indefinitely with the environmental conditions (and perhaps broader economic woes that could materialize) turning away potential buyers and leading to a distressed sale. Tenants may simply be unwilling to consider leasing the property without an adequate build-out. As well, a limited partner who cannot or will not fund in case of a capital call might see his or her investment diluted by the sponsor or another party that provides the necessary funds.

Another point to be made on this unusual deal is that an investor must clarify whether the promote structure links the performance of the two properties or not. The sponsor is incentivized to try to receive performance fees on a standalone basis so that if one property does very well (the retail property, most likely) the sponsor promote will be calculated based on that property's performance alone. Any arrangement can be negotiated but a structure which involves a parallel promote structure for both properties but calculates the promote on a standalone basis is very sponsor-friendly. Such a structure would probably ensure a healthy performance fee for the sponsor after the retail property is sold and then much less reward for operating the industrial property for several years after acquisition.

The investor should prefer that the reward calculation ties the properties performance to each other.

In short, if investors knew that the industrial tenant would remain current on its rent for many years (without using its newfound leverage to renegotiate the lease), this would be a much more attractive deal. But given the challenges the business is facing, the potential return probably does not compensate for the risk, especially considering the environmental challenges which may turn away tenants, limit site utilization options, and reduce value to a seller or lender. Moreover, the sponsor's bold assumptions about (1) the working capital needs of the deal, (2) the tenant's likelihood of staying in the space, and (3) the costs involved in leasing the vacant and potentially vacant space do not seem conservative enough to be relied upon by investors. At the minimum, the investor should adjust the projections using more realistic or more conservative assumptions and evaluate the deal using the resulting projections.

Post-commentary Notes

....

....

....

....

....

....

....

....

....

....

....

....

....

....

The Offering Memorandum as an Advocacy Document
Some limited partnership investors are surprised to
discover that they need to scrutinize investments
offerings; while investors may have thought that the
document was primarily a presentation of facts, they will
soon discover it is actually a document making an
argument. While investments in property might often be
simpler than investments in operating businesses, there
are still plenty of moving parts and assumptions that play
a role in a realistic projection of returns. The sponsor may
not be incentivized to produce a document that covers all
of the bases if investors do not demand such a thorough
presentation. Rather, the sponsor may provide a simple
set of photos and projections that advances the following
argument: (a) this project has a projected rate of return
that is attractive, (b) the business plan is simple and we
are qualified to carry it out, and (c) while there are always
risks—especially broad economic risks—you can rest
assured that this is a relatively safe bet. But all projections
rely on assumptions and sometimes the offering is not
fully transparent about which assumptions went into the
projections and how strong those assumptions are.

Below are five examples of ways that an offering
memorandum may advance the sponsor's argument that
the investment is a good one:

1. Maps. Maps are often included in the offering
memorandum in order to demonstrate proximity to public
transportation, major transportation arteries, and nearby
properties of note (e.g., a major retailer, employer, or
cultural institution). These maps give a sense that the

property's location is desirable to tenants in the submarket being served. But maps may hide more than they reveal.

An offering memorandum soliciting investments in multifamily property in New York City's Washington Heights, for example, might include a map showing how close the property is to Broadway retail and the 1 subway line (see image below). Google maps lists the distance from 636 Fort Washington Avenue to Key Food, a supermarket at 4365 Broadway, at 5 minutes for 0.3 miles. But the map does not show that 636 Fort Washington is located on a hill (thus, Washington "Heights"), making the uphill walk back home from the supermarket or subway much more challenging for tenants, and perhaps impossible for elderly or disabled tenants. (One mapping tool pegged the difference in elevation between the property and Key Food at 150 feet!)

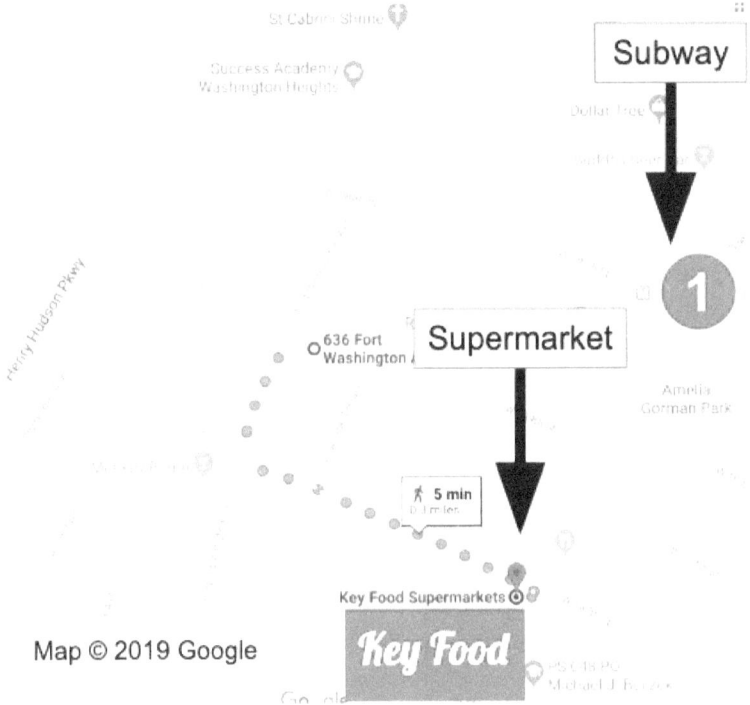

Map © 2019 Google

Some questions to consider when looking at maps include:

(a) despite proximity to notable landmarks or amenities, are there natural barriers such as topography, traffic controls (one-way street, traffic lights, etc.), or dangerous neighborhoods, that restrict quick and easy travel among the points on the map? "It's right next too..." may not tell the whole story; one offering memorandum boasted a property's location score[2] (it was high because the property was in a densely-populated city) but a simple

---

[2] A standardized way to measure how convenient a property's location is, several companies rate property scores based on factors such as access to public transportation and entertainment.

google search revealed a 16-minute walk to the closest subway stop through a crime-ridden area; sometimes there is a difference of only a few blocks that determines whether a location is safe or unsafe, beautiful or unkempt, and convenient or inconvenient.

(b) do the physical condition and unique characteristics of the subject property make it inaccessible to the desired tenants? There may be zoning restrictions, tenancy or co-tenancy conditions, physical restrictions, and even historical-reputational issues that might make it very difficult to attract tenants or make desired changes at the property. For example, a very old building might need a costly upgrade to its electrical systems that would make it cost prohibitive to prepare the building for the tenants being sought for the property.

2. Photos. Property photos are usually included in offering memoranda so that investors will be able to visualize what they might be buying. Photos are especially tricky because there are so many angles and ways to take photos (and edit them) that it can be challenging for anyone to give a sense of a property given all of the unique elements in the units, common areas, and grounds. Moreover, property rents are usually achieved based on the property's offerings relative to the tenants' other options. That means that an old and unkempt apartment building might still command a very high rent if that rent is the lowest rent in the well-located neighborhood. The opposite is also true: very nice properties can struggle to reach profitability if the market rents are low and the property was purchased at a price that was too high.

Seeing photos of a beautiful pool or loading dock at a property may not mean much if the competing properties are in higher demand because they are better-located or have other amenities that the subject property does not have.

Finally, the property condition being displayed in a series of photos does not necessarily represent significant value to a deal. For example, lower-budget items like new paint and shrubbery may indeed represent a well-managed property but it might not make a difference to the experience or economics of certain commercial tenants. In contrast, a photo showing a brand new roof on a very large warehouse or a new parking lot at a regional mall could represent hundreds of thousands of dollars of value and many years of lower maintenance and replacement costs. Moreover, unique architecture, historic facades, or special amenities might be beautiful to look at but might represent high maintenance costs that a new owner will inherit after acquisition. The photos can certainly provide valuable information but prospective investors should consider how the photos substantiate or undermine the arguments made in the investment offering.

3. Area culture and demographics. Demographics might be discussed in order to advance the argument that the property is in a desirable location. This information is often culled from brokerage houses incentivized to encourage transaction activity by painting a rosy picture of the area. Alternatively, this information is sometimes sourced from the local or regional chamber of commerce which provides interesting but not very useful information (e.g., "St. Louis is the 20th largest Metropolitan Statistical Area in the USA with over 2.8 million people as of 2010"). These organizations are also organized to bring business to the area, not to paint an accurate picture of investment potential. Sometimes, area information is misleading, focusing on the strength of local demand ("New grocers in the area include Walmart Neighborhood Market, Wegmans, and Costco") but not describing the excess of retail space in the area that has brought down prices. Indeed, a new lease celebrated by the local community might have actually been signed as a result of generous tax abatements or low rents in the area, conditions that helped the business but might not represent a favorable environment for investors.

4. Comparable sales and leases. Rent comparables are critical for forecasting attainable rents and are sometimes included in investment offerings. However, they are some of the easiest pieces of information to manipulate because it is rare that two locations offer the same value to tenants. Sponsors can cherry-pick the highest rents without providing details that would reveal the superior buildout, terms, or location which justified those high rents at other properties. It is also easy to rationalize the omission of many lower-rent comparables because those properties probably offer less that the subject property in terms of amenities, terms, or location. Although these comparisons are difficult to do, they are most useful when combined with an analysis of the degree of difference ("a 20% better product in a similar location but 50% higher rents").

	Rolling Meadows		Cedar Village (Current)	
	Avg. Unit Size	Avg. Rent	Avg. Unit Size	Avg. Rent
Studio	740	$1,033	695	$830
1 BR	1,225	$1,290	1,300	$1,005
2 BR	1,500	$1,540	1,550	$1,285

5. Market supply and demand information. Sometimes, an offering memorandum will describe new developments in the area in order to share the excitement of the changes happening in the market. Development can certainly indicate a future economy that is more vibrant and active than today's economy. But it can also indicate oversupply, reduced rents, and challenges including overwhelmed public infrastructure (traffic, sewer systems, etc.). Development pipelines are most useful when offered alongside demand surveys and detailed information about the projected rents and offerings of the new developments. For example, an offering memorandum for a multifamily acquisition might mention that there is no new development happening in the area, a condition that will help the property maintain its competitive position. However, this is only true if demand is staying the same or growing (or if supply is shrinking alongside a reduction in demand). If the subject area depends on a nearby military facility for a significant portion of housing and entertainment spending and the military recently announced a reduction in the importance of that facility, demand may be on the way down. Even though supply may not be growing, the demand for the subject property's space—and thus its ability to maintain or increase rents—may be lower in the near future.

A Simple Framework for Evaluating Investment Opportunities

A thoughtful review of an offering memorandum can be accomplished in two steps.

Step 1: Start by reviewing the document line-by-line, taking the projections at face value and making sure you understand the business plan. Make sure to consider the risks that exist as part of the project. For example, in Case 2 above, the proposed project involves: (a) buying an industrial property with a struggling commercial tenant, collecting rent for a few years, and then selling it; and (b) buying a vacant retail property, leasing some of the space, and then quickly selling it to a large company. The industrial acquisition features risks mostly involving the tenant going out of business or demanding a reduction in. Attracting a new tenant and dealing with a period of vacancy could be extremely expensive—requiring money that has not been set aside at the time of acquisition. This adds the extra risk of non-availability of funds for required property repositioning and leasing costs. The retail acquisition features risks including a very short timeline for lease-up in order to sell to the large buyer; as well, leasing space in a completely vacant building is harder than in a mostly-full building. Holding the industrial property for several years presents market risk because in a recession, the tenant might go bankrupt and there may be fewer tenants and buyers interested in the large building. All of the risks above involve understanding the project as presented, without subjecting any assumptions to a critical analysis. The risks are not unique to this project but are much more acute and important than the risks involved when buying a property 100% leased to a tenant with great credit. In that case, the low risk of the tenant going bankrupt or non-renewing is the only risk and is a risk much less likely to materialize than the risks in Case 2 above.

Step 2: Use a critical eye to review the document again and look for information that might demonstrate hidden risks, unrealistic assumptions, or an inconsistent story. For example, in Case 1, the sponsor planned to add washing machines to the apartments as part of a redevelopment. However, the water bills were projected to stay the same as pre-renovation. Using a critical eye means building (or hiring someone to build) an adjusted pro forma with various rents, timelines, and exit cap rates so that you can understand the project's expected returns under a set of assumptions that you are more comfortable with. You may find that a "fantastic" off-market deal may not be so great and "conservative" underwriting may not so realistic after all.

Case 3: Mel Green's Diner: Mixed-use ground-up development

This case features a ground-up development project and a discussion of various types of limited partnership investors, each with a particular appetite for investment risks and opportunities. While reading, consider the following questions:

1. Would you be interested in investing in this deal? If so, at what price and on what terms?

2. What concerns do you have about the deal? What information might you obtain that would satisfy those concerns?

3. What are your own current and anticipated needs as an investor and how are those needs met (or not met) by the proposed project? What would need to change about the deal for you to be comfortable moving forward as a limited partnership investor in this deal?

Overview – Business Plan – Exhibits – Pre-commentary Notes – Commentary – Pre-commentary Notes

Overview

Address: 1515 Broadway, Smithtown, OH 44118

Size: 80,000 square feet parcel (150 feet of frontage on Broadway)

Current occupancy: 100% occupied since 1936, to be delivered vacant

Construction: 1911 (substantially renovated in 1950 and 1995)

Purchase Price: $10.5 million

Total project capitalization: $76.6 million

Equity being sought by sponsor: $49.94 million

Anticipated investment term: five years

Projected return to limited partners: 18.7%

1515 Broadway, Smithtown, OH 44118, Mel Green's Diner — the development site.

Mel Green's Diner has been an important Smithtown spot for taxi drivers, police officers, and high school students to grab a bite for over 80 years. Located on the edge of Smithtown, its nearly two-acre parcel has made it easy for sports-team busses to drop in, not to mention countless minivans. Twice per year for many years, the Diner hosted a community carnival that drew visitors from throughout the county. Because of the hot property market in Smithtown and the new train stop ten blocks east of the diner, the property is ripe for development. The sponsor has put the property under contract for $10.5MM and plans to develop an office building on the site with the premier national convenience store chain occupying the retail portions of floors one and two. The sponsor's personal relationship with the owner of the property and with the head of the convenience store's real estate department allowed for this great deal to come together quickly. Moreover, the sponsor's personal relationship with XO Leveraged Construction, a major international builder, resulted in a favorable contract for a very high-end design and build agreement, at only $350 per square foot. Preliminary loan terms have been negotiated with a local lender to extend a three-year construction loan by two years assuming certain leasing benchmarks are achieved. XO intends to use advanced modular construction technology to keep costs very low by pre-fabricating much of the construction at an off-site facility.

The Diner site is not far from the corporate headquarters of 3Eyes, a major digital surveillance products developer. 3Eyes relocated to the area around ten years ago and has been a catalyst for economic growth in the area. Many software companies—especially startups in the data security space—have followed 3Eyes to the Smithtown area. There are four other Class A office buildings in this submarket, all built in the last ten years with property tax incentives. The buildings, ranging from 30,000 to 200,000 square feet, average 96% occupancy and many service software company tenants. Although the property tax incentive program has ended, new tenants coming to the area are settling for less-than-adequate offices and are seeking high-end space. Ultimately, SCU—a great software engineering college nearby—should drive great job growth in the area as companies seek to capitalize on a young and talented labor pool as well as the relatively low cost of living in the area.

Business Plan

The sponsor proposes to build a six-story, 150,000 square foot, mixed-use facility, with 130,000 square foot of office space and 20,000 square feet of retail pre-leased to the premier national convenience store chain (name available upon request). Of 350 parking spaces, 90 are designated for convenience store use. The retail space has been pre-leased at $80 per square foot, with rent to commence one year after the sponsor finishes the tenant buildout to the required specifications. This one year free rent period is expected to begin at the end of year two. The lease is for ten years without rental increases and the retail tenant has six fixed-rate renewal options, each for five years with a 10% step-up in rent each time a renewal period commences.

Development costs are estimated to be $350 per square foot, per the design-build contract, totalling $76.6 million. The retail tenant is expected to take occupancy two years after acquisition—before the construction on the building is completed—and office tenants are projected to move in starting at the end of year three.

Based on an analysis of office demand, new construction, and absorption, the property is expected to achieve 50%, 70%, and 90% occupancy of the office component at the end of year three, four, and five, respectively, at then-current market rents, currently at $70 per square foot. Rents are assumed to grow 2% annually. Because the building will be built with state-of-the-art utility metering equipment, the sponsor projects that tenants will pay all utilities, including water and sewer.

Exhibit 1: Development rendering

Rendering of new development: office floors three to six (Microsoft logo for display purposes only—we have had no specific conversations with Microsoft to tenant the property).

Exhibit 2: Diner local map

Exhibit 3: Diner regional map with location pins of similarly-situated properties

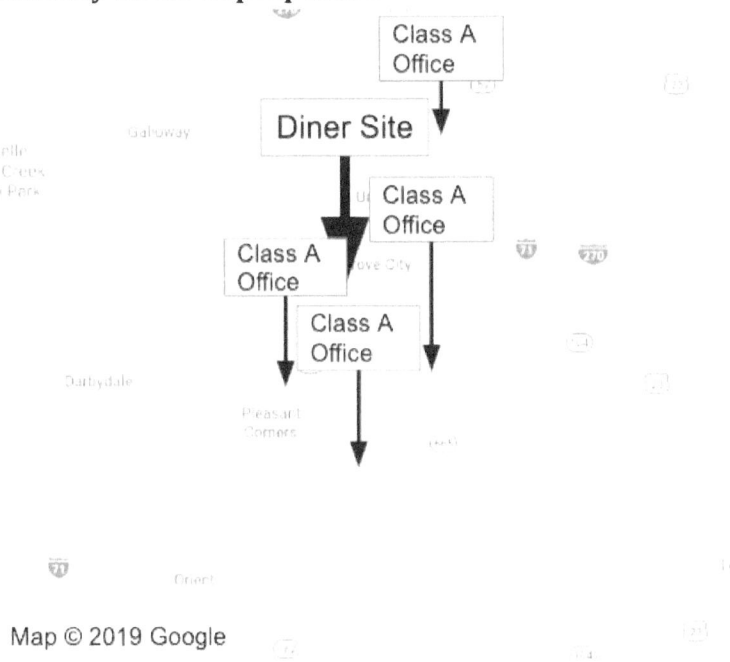

Map © 2019 Google

Exhibit 4: General assumptions

Assumptions

Development Cost	$350	psf
Total size	150,000	sf
Office portion size	130,000	sf
Retail portion size	20,000	sf
Rent Growth	2%	
Expense Growth	2%	
Monthly Parking Rent	$130	per space
Office Rent	$70.00	psf
Walgreens Rent	$80.00	psf
Interest	7%	
Combined Loan Term	5	years
Amortization	15	years

Exhibit 5: Rent and occupancy assumptions over time

	Year 0	Year 1	Year 2	Year 3	Year 4	Year 5	Year 6
Walgreens Rent	$80.00	$80.00	$80.00	$80.00	$80.00	$80.00	$80.00
Office Rent	$70.00	$71.40	$72.83	$74.28	$75.77	$77.29	$78.83
Office Occupancy	0%	0%	0%	0%	50%	70%	90%

Exhibit 6: Sources and uses

Sources

Sponsor Equity	$7,660,000	10.0%
LP Equity	$49,940,000	65.2%
Debt	$19,000,000	24.8%
Total	$76,600,000	

Uses

Purchase Price	$10,500,000
Closing Expenses	$600,000
Development	$52,500,000
Acquisition Fee	$1,000,000
Interest Reserve	$12,000,000
Total	$76,600,000

Exhibit 7: Promote structure

Waterfall

	LP	Sponsor	Hurdle
Return of Capital	90%	10%	12%
Hurdle 1	65%	35%	16%
Hurdle 2	50%	50%	

Exhibit 8: Pro forma income, expense, and cash flow

	Year 0	Year 1	Year 2	Year 3	Year 4	Year 5
Walgreens Rent		$0	$0	$0	$1,600,000	$1,600,000
Office Rent		$0	$0	$0	$4,925,066	$7,032,995
Office Parking Income		$0	$0	$0	$202,800	$283,920
Net Rental Income		**$0**	**$0**	**$0**	**$6,727,866**	**$8,916,915**
Property Tax (Unreimbursed Portion)		$300,000	$306,000	$312,120	$624,000	$381,888
Insurance		$150,066	$153,067	$156,129	$50,000	$51,000
Electric and Gas		$29,000	$25,000	$80,000	$40,000	$0
Water		$14,500	$12,500	$40,000	$20,000	$0
Property Management Fee		$0	$0	$0	$336,393	$445,846
Constr. Mgmt (Dev. budget)		$0	$0	$0	$0	$0
Payroll + Contractor (Dev. budget)		$0	$0	$0	$0	$0
Repair and Maintenance		$0	$0	$0	$75,000	$80,000
Leasing Commissions		$0	$0	$0	$0	$0
Interest		$2,049,330	$2,049,330	$2,049,330	$2,049,330	$2,049,330
Other - plug		$50,000	$51,000	$52,020	$53,060	$54,122
Total Expenses		**$2,592,896**	**$2,596,897**	**$2,689,599**	**$3,247,784**	**$3,062,185**
Net Operating Income		-$2,592,896	-$2,596,897	-$2,689,599	$3,480,083	$5,854,729
Exit Value @ 5.50% CAP						$187,487,795
Exit Value @ 5.00% CAP						$206,236,575
Exit Value @ 4.50% CAP						$229,151,750
Principal Balance						$14,708,430
Return of Interest Reserve						$4,120,608
Cash Flow (levered, deal-level)	-$76,600,000	0	0	0	$3,480,083	$201,503,482

Exhibit 9: Pro forma returns projection post-waterfall

Returns Summary

LP Total Cash Flow	-$68.940,000	$0	$0	$0	$3.132.074	$158.539.221
LP Cumulative Cash Flow	-$68.940,000	-$68,940.000	-$68,940.000	-$68.940.000	-$65.807,926	$92.731,296
LP IRR	18.7%					
LP Equity Multiple	2.35 x					
LP Peak Equity	$68.940.000					
LP Profit	$92.731,296					
Sponsor Total Cash Flow	-$7.660.000	$0	$0	$0	$348,008	$42.964.261
Sponsor Cumulative Cash Flow	-$7.660.000	-$7,660.000	-$7,660.000	-$7.660.000	-$7.311.992	$35.652,269
Sponsor IRR	41.5%					
Sponsor Equity Multiple	5.65 x					
Sponsor Peak Equity	$7.660.000					
Sponsor Profit	$35.652,269					

Pre-commentary Notes

....

....

....

....

....

....

....

....

....

....

....

....

....

....

Case Study 3 Commentary:
Initially, this seems like an impressive deal—a great credit tenant has already signed a lease and the sponsor seems to have the relationships to make things happen. High quality builder, high-end building, and good-credit retail tenant. And a projected return of over 21% at the project level and around 18% to the limited partner with the

ability to invest a substantial sum (around $50 million).
But are the projections realistic? Whatever the projections
might be after some adjusted assumptions are layered into
the model, which risks are being taken in the hopes of
receiving those projected returns?

First, property taxes on new development can turn a great
project into one that does not make a sufficient return.
The fact that all of the competing product in the market
was built with generous property tax incentives that are
no longer available means that their cost structure is
probably much more healthy than that of this project. In a
competitive scenario without enough tenants to fill all of
the Class A space, the other projects will be able to offer
lower rents in order to compete for tenants. A shrewd
investor will need to understand how the property tax
estimates were obtained. Was a tax consultant hired?
What is the range of possible values for the tax and what
does that do to returns? For example, maybe assessed
value on new construction in Smithtown is based on an
estimate of construction costs and the property tax rate is
3.96% of market values.[3] If that is the case, the only value
to estimate is the range of estimated construction costs
the taxing authority will place on the property. Moreover,
if the tax assessor has access to the actual costs for the

---

[3] This rate would be at the higher end of property tax rates for
commercial properties in the United States. For a sense of
commercial property tax rates across the United States, see
page three of *50-State Property Tax Comparison Study (2018)*,
Lincoln Institute of Land Policy and Minnesota Center for Fiscal
Excellence.
https://www.lincolninst.edu/sites/default/files/pubfiles/50-state-
property-tax-comparison-for-2017-full_1.pdf

project, there may be a fairly certain estimate of property taxes that will be assessed upon project completion.

Developers often look at cost structures of other projects when planning a new project. For example, an office building developer might estimate that a new project, like other projects it has developed, will have operating expenses of one third (33%) of rental income. And that may be true in jurisdictions with lower property tax costs. But the property built in a higher property tax jurisdiction could have a completely different cost structure. The subject property, according to the pro forma in the investment offering, can generate around 15% of construction costs in annual rent (PGI of around $11MM divided by $72.4MM, the expected construction cost after returning excess interest reserve). But 3.96% of its construction value must be paid in property tax, translating to over 25% of its rents being paid out in property taxes alone. In contrast, a jurisdiction with property tax rates of 1-2% of market value will require an allocation of only 6-12% of rents to go to property taxes. Here, pro forma rents in year four—presumably raised after a post-construction reassessment—are $1,248,000 (calculated by recognizing that the $624,000 is the unreimbursed portion and the occupancy assumption is 50%), around 1.5% of the all-in construction cost estimate. Without yet knowing how Smithtown does its property tax assessments or what the tax rates are, we might look at the year 1 property tax estimate of $325,000, around 3.1% of the acquisition price for the building. Applying that rate to the estimated post-construction market value of $72,400,000 (again, after adding back unused interest reserve and assuming this is how the assessor will approach things), property taxes should be $2,244,400, or $996,400 more than currently budgeted, an increase corresponding to almost 9% of projected stabilized income.

Next, how deep is the market for tenants willing to pay $70 per square foot for office space in a market that likely has much cheaper options available? (It is safe to assume there are cheaper options because the offering memorandum describes the subject project as brand new, "Class A" office space.) It is exciting to think about new businesses coming to the market but most startups do not have much money available to pay salaries let alone Class A rents when there are inexpensive options nearby. The rents charged in the market will need to be understood before assuming that the project can be leased relatively quickly at $70 per foot or more. Note: the model really assumes rents even higher than $70 per square foot. Because the sponsor projects significant "office parking income" at the property, s/he is really assuming higher office rents because suburban office landlords often provide parking to tenants at no extra charge[4] according to the number of square feet leased (e.g., three spaces per thousand square feet of space leased). Year six income is the first stabilized year at 90% occupancy and office parking income in that year comprises around 4% of the

---

[4] See for brief discussion page 57 of Brian Miller and Robert Miller's *Timing Your Office Lease: a Timeline for Saving Thousands of Dollars Finding & Negotiating Office Space: Counting down the Months until the End of Your Lease!* (Trafford, 2004.)

office rent amount. This means that the $70 per square foot rent assumption (with 2% annual growth assumed) is really almost $73 per square foot. Moreover, no free rent, tenant improvement allowance, or leasing commissions were projected in the model. Assuming that all of these would be factors in a successful lease negotiation, the model should account for a lower net rent if the costs are not accounted for elsewhere. Finally, while property tax increases are often reimbursed by office tenants, property taxes are usually paid by the landlord. This large reimbursement assumption needs to be subjected to research: how does the sponsor know the tenants will pay that large cost as well? The way the reimbursements seem to be calculated—although lacking the original excel makes it challenging to know for sure—also has 90% of the property taxes paid by the 90% office occupancy. If this is actually the case, the office tenants are projected to pay for retail tenant property taxes, an unlikely scenario to say the least. Perhaps there is more to this story and the retail tenant pays a certain portion directly. Or maybe there was an error in the model. A sharp investor will ask about this.

The retail space seems to offer a safe and favorable return—certainly the fact that the space is pre-leased gives reason to trust the developer. However, there are important factors to consider here. First, the landlord is responsible for the tenant buildout which means that any build-out delays are at the landlord's expense since rent payments do not commence until 12 months after move-in which follows the completion of the buildout. As well, the entire project's reliance on modular construction should be understood as well. Modular construction offers the promise of fewer weather-related construction delays and lower costs, but any risks should be evaluated.

The following model tries to present a more conservative set of projections for the project. This new set of projections only gives a rough indication of where returns might actually end up. It is impossible to predict, of course, and more investigation is warranted in order to get better informed (on property taxes, for example). Of course, more information might lead to further reductions in projected returns. However, further research might substantiate some of the sponsor's projections (or lead to increases in expected returns)—for example, by reading through a property tax consultant's report justifying the $1,248,000 property tax assumption in the pro forma.

The below exhibits are based on an adjusted model which:
a) Assumes no rent in year four to better account for construction delays, free rent, tenant improvements and leasing commissions (both represented by lost rent instead of paid out expense) but assumes the property tax reassessment is delayed to year five as well
b) Removes parking income
c) Increases projected property taxes in year four to $2,244,400, or 3.1% of the construction cost for the new building, an increase of $996,400 over the currently-modeled amount and assumes that the only property taxes that are reimbursed correspond to 40% of the office occupancy percentage (i.e., 36% of the taxes when office occupancy is at 90%)
d) Increases exit cap assumption by 100 bps to 6.00% CAP

e) Reduces office market rent assumption from $70.00 to $63.00 (10% decrease). Note: the model assumes that this number increases by 2% per year both for vacant space (anticipated market rents) and occupied space (contract rent bumps). This $63.00 assumption rises to around $70 by year five of the model (see below).

	Year 0	Year 1	Year 2	Year 3	Year 4	Year 5	Year 6
Market Rent	$63.00	$64.26	$65.55	$66.86	$68.19	$69.56	$70.95

Exhibit 9: Revised pro forma with more conservative assumptions

Returns Summary

LP Total Cash Flow	-$68,940,000	$0	$0	$0	$0	$107,743,210
LP Cumulative Cash Flow	-$68,940,000	-$68,940,000	-$68,940,000	-$68,940,000	-$68,940,000	$38,803,210
LP IRR	9.3%					
LP Equity Multiple	1.56 x					
LP Peak Equity	$68,940,000					
LP Profit	$38,803,210					
Sponsor Total Cash Flow	-$7,660,000	$0	$0	$0	$0	$11,971,468
Sponsor Cumulative Cash Flow	-$7,660,000	-$7,660,000	-$7,660,000	-$7,660,000	-$7,660,000	$4,311,468
Sponsor IRR	9.3%					
Sponsor Equity Multiple	1.56 x					
Sponsor Peak Equity	$7,660,000					
Sponsor Profit	$4,311,468					

Exhibit 10: A comparison of original and revised cash flow and deal level IRR projections

	Year 0	Year 1	Year 2	Year 3	Year 4	Year 5	IRR
CF (levered, deal-level)	-$76,600,000	$0	$0	$0	$3,480,083	$201,503,482	21.85%
Adjusted CF	-$76,600,000	$0	$0	$0	$0	$119,714,677	9.34%

The results under the revised figures are not pretty. The deal reaches only slightly exceeds a 9% IRR and, as a result, the sponsor does not reach any of the waterfall hurdles. Aside from the healthy acquisition fee, the sponsor does not receive anything that the limited partner does not (aside from some fee income, perhaps, depending on how involved the sponsor is in construction and property management—note, however, that the offering memorandum makes no mention of sponsor involvement in construction or project management before the building is completed). One positive element of this deal is the alignment of interests between the sponsor and the limited partner given the high return hurdles and the large (10%) equity interest provided by the sponsor, a large sum and percentage of the deal. This "skin in the game" should cause the sponsor to use all available resources to get the deal done successfully and quickly even if the returns are below the waterfall hurdles.

Like in any deal, the limited partner must decide what pro forma is compelling given the available facts and then, based on that pro forma—and not the one circulated by the sponsor—make decisions about investing. The assumptions used in the adjusted model were just for illustrative purposes, of course. Projected office rents (and concessions) should be based on some market knowledge and the construction costs and schedule should also be based on comparable projects and conversations with experts. As an exercise in tempering what seem to be very aggressive assumptions by the sponsor here, however, there is much value in using an adjusted model like this one when making the choice of whether to invest and how much. Ultimately, one incorrect or overly optimistic assumption (such as the assumption about property taxes) can make a deal uneconomical despite having many attractive elements. Remember, this adjusted model is not a "downside" scenario in which things do not go well, an economic downturn results, etc. This is a more conservative "successful" scenario of project completion and lease-up. If these were the assumptions that fit with an investor's sense of the market and project type, the investor would then be well-advised to consider whether the projected 9.34% return adequately compensates for the risk of construction delays and cost increases, unexpected leasing challenges and costs, and the results of broader economic issues.

Post-commentary Notes

....
....
....
....
....
....
....
....
....
....
....
....
....
....

How Different Kinds of Investors can Evaluate Limited
Partnership Investing

Each investor has unique risk tolerances that stem from
his or her values, life goals, and needs. Certain expenses
that may come up in the near or distant future may dictate
how liquid (how easily convertible to cash at a reasonable
price) the investor's investments need to be. The amount

of money available to the investor may also influence the perceived risks the investor is willing to take. As well, the makeup of the investor's portfolio may impact future investments decisions. For example, if an investor has a significant amount of money invested in technology stocks, he or she might not be as interested in investments in real estate investments with high-tech companies as tenants because headwinds in the technology space might make a severe impact on the investor's net worth. Investment horizons might also be important—if a significant amount of a person's net worth is invested in two projects that are both projected to return capital in seven years or more, the investor may face liquidity issues if he or she expects to face large personal expenses in three to five years.

A. Wealth and Liquidity

An investor's level of wealth and liquidity is very relevant to his or her investment decision making. For example, investors should consider how likely it is that their LP investment will need a capital call—a cash infusion by investors. (Case 2 above was one such project at project at risk of needing one.) If an investor does not have the funds available to make such a capital call, his/her interest could be diluted by the sponsor or another investor who puts up the needed capital. Furthermore, LP investors have very little control of the partnership decisions and years can go by without any cash distributions (even when the partnership is profitable). This can result in "phantom" taxes, tax liabilities to investors based on the income of the property owned by the partnership even though no cash is distributed by the partnership. An LP investor will need to have enough money to pay these tax bills in order to avoid tax delinquency. This is especially important because there is not a deep market for LP interests given the control issues involved which means that an investor who needs to sell his or her LP interest will probably need to sell at a steep discount.

B. Leverage in a Negotiation with a Sponsor

Some limited partners bring much to the table when negotiating with a sponsor. A wealthy investor may be able to fund most or all of the needed capital for a project, saving the sponsor time and effort in fundraising and communicating with investors. An experienced or well-connected investor might help the sponsor find other investors, connect with important service providers, or execute certain elements of the business plan. But investors without much to offer should consider why they are being offered the deal in the first place: are smarter investors shunning the deal because they know enough to be nervous? An investor's leverage can result in a more favorable waterfall structure (whether in terms of a lower promote, higher hurdle, or more sponsor equity invested to improve the incentive structure), better reporting depth and frequency, or more protections for the limited partner.

C. Emotional, Budgetary, and Cultural Aspects

Investors must consider what will happen if the projected returns do not materialize or if there is a permanent loss of principal. Will they face stress and health issues? Is the amount invested small relative to their income or net worth? Private investments are by their nature less transparent and more person-dependant than, say, investments in blue-chip stocks. They are also less liquid which means that despite an urgent need or demand to sell one's shares, there may be no buyer, even for ten cents on the dollar. Even in a global recession, customers around the world will probably continue buying soft drinks, helping beverage companies to maintain their value to a large extent. However, a building under construction that was not pre-leased may face years of vacancy and losses if the economy dips before leases can be signed. How will your family, your emotional state, and your wallet fare under that scenario? Some investors certainly have an acute sense that they are "losing money" when it is not invested and are "risk friendly." Others fear loss of principal invested more than anything else. Thankfully, there are many kinds of investments, each with its own flavor of risk, liquidity, and potential returns. Even if real estate investing as a limited partner is a good fit for you given your financial position and goals, certain geographies, business plans, and sponsors might be a better fit than others.